STINKERS AND STINGERS

LEVEL **3** READER

READING LEVEL · GRADES 2 TO 4

Copyright ©2010 Creative Edge, LLC. All rights reserved.
Printed in Guangzhou, Guangdong, China.

Written by Kathryn Knight

Saddled with Stingers

Do you think creeping critters are interesting and fun to watch? Beware! Many insects, spiders, and other crawlers have ways of keeping unwanted guests—like you—away. They sting, bite, pinch, spray, or make quite a stink!

This cute caterpillar may look harmless, but those spines are painful stingers. The venomous prick from a saddleback caterpillar can hurt for days. No one messes with *this* baby moth.

Sibine stimulea of eastern North America fools predators because it looks like it has two heads.

You Little Stinker!

This pudgy little fellow is a stinker! If a bird or lizard gets too close, the swallowtail caterpillar pops up its orange-colored *osmeteria* (oz-mih-**teer**-ee-uh) behind its head. These organs release a very smelly substance. It is so awful that predators will steer clear. Sometimes a bad smell can be just as effective as a bad sting.

The caterpillars of the Papilionidae family turn into some of the most beautiful (and harmless) butterflies in the world.

Gentle Giant

Watch out! This big hairy spider must have quite a bite—right? Not really. The tarantula's venom is weaker than a bee's sting and harmless to humans who are not allergic. In fact, many tarantulas are kept as pets. (If bothered, they *will* bite—and their barbed hairs can also stick you and make you itch.) They eat mainly insects, but the largest tarantulas will hunt frogs, mice, and small birds. Some live in silk-lined borrows. Others live in trees, waiting for a small victim to walk by.

Some tarantulas are small enough to span a quarter. The largest, the goliath birdeater, has a 4-inch body and a 12-inch leg span. It could stretch across a dinner plate!

Beware the Tail!

Some of the most dreaded stingers in the world are scorpions. No one wants to see one of these fellows scuttling near. The claws look fierce, but it's the barb on the tail that will get you.

The venom in a scorpion's stinger can kill a small animal. The scorpion uses its sting to kill its prey, but it will also sting in self-defense. Many reptiles, birds, and small mammals that thought a scorpion looked like a tasty meal have suffered from its sting. Very few scorpions are actually dangerous to people. But the sting still hurts!

Scorpions are arachnids, like ticks and spiders. They have two main body parts and eight legs. Scorpions are found worldwide. Yikes!

Hold Your Nose!

Some of the most dreaded stinkers in the world are shield bugs. In fact, most people call them stinkbugs. They are named for their shape (they look like shields), but these bugs are also shielded by a mighty weapon. They release a liquid that smells horrendous. If you've ever disturbed a shield bug, you know the smell. Ugh!

Shield bugs belong to the order of "true bugs." After they release their smelly liquid, the stink can stay on a plant for quite a while. Pee-yew!

Some shield bugs are brown or green. Others are colorful. They all have piercing mouthparts that sink into leaves and plants to suck the juices. They have no claws or pinchers. Yet very few animals will prey on shield bugs. They smell and taste so bad that most birds will spit them out.

If you see a gray baglike nest in a tree or on a building, don't touch it! It could be a nest of hornets. You don't want to mess with these big wasps. They have one of the most venomous and painful stings of the insect world. If a hornet thinks you will disturb the nest, it will attack—and so will its buddies!

The bald-faced hornet is common in the United States. The largest hornet, the Asian giant hornet, is one of the most venomous insects on Earth.

Hornets release an "alarm" chemical that tells other hornets to attack. If you see a hornet in your yard, don't kill it without checking to see if there is a nest nearby. Otherwise, the dying hornet will send up the alarm and you'll be chased by angry hornets with fierce stingers!

You would think that an earwig could keep any predator away just by waving its sharp pincers. But there are plenty of birds, reptiles, and bigger bugs that try to dine on earwigs. So an earwig uses another defense. It gives off a very foul smell and taste if it is bitten or squished. A hungry lizard that suffers one taste of earwig may stay away from others.

Toxic Milk

The lovely milkweed plant has a white sappy liquid in its stems. This "milk" is bitter and toxic. Some caterpillars, such as the monarch caterpillar, are able to eat the leaves without getting sick. The poison collects in the caterpillar's body. Predators learn to avoid these caterpillars (and the bitter butterflies they become). Why have a poisonous sting when your whole body can be poisonous?

Southern Fire

The United States has been invaded! Red fire ants from South America came to Alabama about 80 years ago—and stayed! These ferocious ants build large nests in  the soil, and they don't like visitors. Any animal that wanders near their mound will be swarmed. And these ants bite—*and* sting! Fire ants can quickly cover and kill a bird or small mammal.

One fire ant can sting its victim again and again. It bites down with its strong jaws and jabs with its rear stinger. It slides around (still attached) and jabs again. It will move in a complete circle, stinging away, until it is brushed off.

Solenopsis invicta delivers
stings so painful, the skin
feels like it's on fire!

Liquid Stinger

Blister beetles come in many colors and they look rather harmless. They are not harmless. These plant-eating beetles leak *cantharidin*, an oily, poisonous liquid. Cantharidin is often used for removing warts. So you can imagine what this stuff does to healthy, soft skin. It burns the skin and causes it to blister.

The blister beetle's "liquid stinger" delivers a solid jab.

Stay-Away Spray

● ●

Inside the tail end of the bombardier beetle are three small chambers. Two chambers each hold a different harmless chemical. But if the beetle is threatened, the beetle's muscles push the two chemicals into the third chamber where they mix. A chemical reaction takes place. The stinky mixture becomes boiling hot and—*pop!*—sprays out onto the victim's face! This is painful to people, but it can kill small creatures.

The bombardier beetle can move its rear end around to aim deadly steam directly at its victim.

Claws that Sting

Many stinging critters
have claws or strong jaws,
but their sting is in their
back end. Not the centipede.
This many-legged wriggler
grabs its prey with
forcipules (venom claws)
that are located on
either side of its head.
The claws then inject
venom that kills
or stuns the prey.
A centipede's venomous
bite is quite painful to
people, but it is rarely fatal.

Centipedes are not insects.
They are chilopods. They
live in moist areas under
rocks, logs, and leaves.

Furry and Fierce

This cute little furry leaf-eater is a serious threat to trees, eating over one million acres of forest each year. And it's also a threat to your skin! Those fine hairs are little needles that prick and cause pain and rash. This is the gypsy moth caterpillar. It looks harmless, but you should never handle one. In fact, don't handle any caterpillar with hairs. They can—*zing*—sting!

Lovely Lady—with Fangs

The female black widow is a beautiful shiny black or brown color with a red hourglass-shaped mark on her abdomen. The male is much smaller and rarely seen. Do you know why? Because the female often kills and eats the male—making her a widow, indeed.

This spider's bite is quick and sharp. She injects prey with venom through her fangs. She is one of the most venomous spiders, so stay away from this lady.

Scar-y Bite

The brown recluse spider is not very big, and it tends to hide away out of view. But this wispy, pale spider injects venom that is particularly gruesome. It causes *necrosis* (death of tissue cells). The bite area gets worse and worse as the skin is eaten away by the toxin in the venom. It can take months to heal, leaving a deep scar.

The brown recluse is also called the fiddleback or violin spider. Many have a violin-shaped marking, with the neck of the violin pointing to the abdomen.

Stinky, Sticky Goo

Termites are social insects, like bees and ants. Many soldier termites have huge jaws that prevent attacking ants from getting into the termite nest. But the nasute (nay-**soot**) termite soldiers have long snouts. These snouts are hose nozzles. When ants approach, nasutes spray them with a stinky, sticky chemical. This toxic glue stops the enemy in their tracks. Goo-d defense!

Nasute termites live in tropical areas around the world. The soldier's spray-snout is called a nasus (**nay**-suhs), which means nose.

The Exterminator

Many ants sting to defend their nest or attack prey. However, common black ants and carpenter ants have no stingers. Instead they bite and spray.

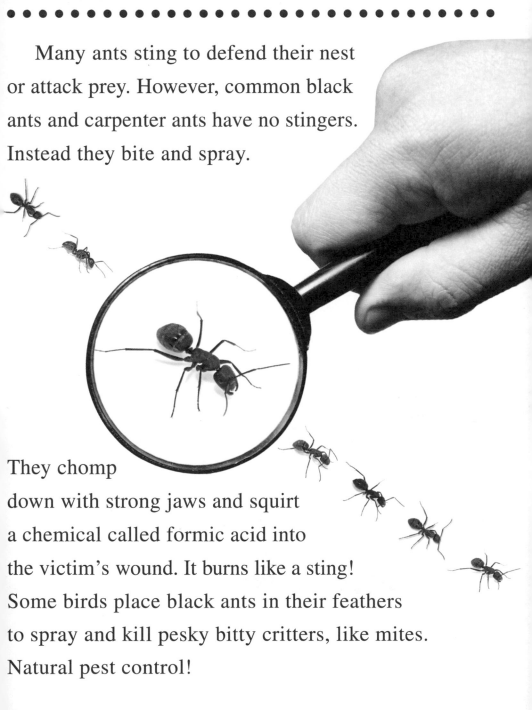

They chomp down with strong jaws and squirt a chemical called formic acid into the victim's wound. It burns like a sting! Some birds place black ants in their feathers to spray and kill pesky bitty critters, like mites. Natural pest control!

Unwelcome Neighbors

Yellow jackets are small wasps. Like larger wasps, yellow jackets sting their victims repeatedly. Unlike most wasps, yellow jackets hang out close to people. They crave the sugar in soda drinks, garbage cans, and picnic foods. So people come into contact with yellow jackets more often than with any other stinging insect. And it hurts!

If you spot a yellow jacket hovering near the ground in your yard, stay away from that spot. It could be the entrance to a nest!

Many yellow jacket nests are underground with one entrance hole. Because of this, people easily mow over or walk past a nest. This sends these fellows into a fury! They will attack and fly after an intruder for a long distance. The unlucky person may run and run and think he's escaped, only to feel those fiery stings!

Stinging Champs

The United States has plenty of stingers and stinkers, but be glad some are *not* here. Bullet ants of South America deliver the most painful sting of the insect world. It is said to be as painful as being shot with a bullet!

A jack jumper ant's sting is so venomous, that in Tasmania, more people die from it than from unfortunate encounters with spiders, snakes, wasps, and sharks combined!

Our many-legged friends may nip us and send up a stink, but they are awesome creatures!

Myrmecia pilosula, the jack jumper of Australia, can leap 2 to 8 inches onto its victim!